The unhappiest one

Finding Joy
in my Journey to Purpose

ISBN: 978-1-7376721-1-1

The unhappiest one

**Finding Joy
in my Journey to Purpose**

dia wall

To my mom, Anita.

For each sacrifice…
For every hard decision…
For your incredible, unconditional support and love…

Thank you. I wouldn't be me without you.

I couldn't love you more.

Table of
Contents

Introduction

You've Got it All

I HAD THIS EXHILARATED DELIRIUM when my little girl was born. Alina. Like so many things in my life, she arrived before I felt quite ready. There was this mixture of overwhelming joy, wonder, gratitude and love, unlike anything I had ever felt in my life. Tears still come to my eyes when I think about the moment when I became a mama.

Soon after, the rhythms of life took over. Three days later, my husband Kevin found me hiding on the floor of my closet sobbing uncontrollably because I was a wreck inside. I haven't told you yet about the painful process to get to my perfect baby girl or the struggles to find my footing once we did. That's why we're here.

I'm in my early thirties, an accomplished professional with a career I dreamed of since I was just nine. Yes, nine years old. I've got a really cute husband who's devoted and generous and kind and funny. He genuinely loves me as I am, deeply and with everything he has. Now, I have the child we prayed for from when we knew that we would be husband and wife, and I am paralyzed.

You know that feeling, don't you?

On the surface, it can seem as if you have it all together and that everything is going your way. In a world where we compare our standing to the place we believe someone else has already arrived, then feel inadequate, I'm here to tell you that all the titles, accomplishments and material things in the universe are not enough.

So that day, on the floor of the closet in our home, with a tiny blessing only three days old, I asked myself the question it seems we've all asked ourselves at some point. I can't promise that I have your answer, but I did find mine.

Why are you the unhappiest one in the room, when youve got it all?

Chapter One

This is Good, But That's Better

I HAIL FROM TEXAS, the land of Friday night lights and the best brisket in the world. A few months after we moved to a Dallas suburb, there was a Labor Day parade. Before I knew it, there they were. The Irving High School drill team came marching down Main Street, clad in their sequin field uniforms, spotless white boots and a matching cowboy hat. I was mesmerized on the spot!

My mom had enrolled me in dance at just three years old. You see, I had three brothers and since our house was often boisterous and a bit rough, she wanted me to get some grace somehow. The thing is, I was awful. I'm not exaggerating. To hear my mom tell it today, I looked like a "plow mule" at my first dance recital. Her eyes always light up when she talks about the smile on my face though.

I loved dance class. Maybe it was the music or the costumes or the ability to express myself in a way that I wasn't able to back then. Either way, dance was my jam.

When I saw those gorgeous girls marching in perfect formation, the drumline rumbling, smiles big as the state of Texas, I knew that I wanted to be one of them one day. I remember asking my mom, "Who are they?" I promised myself that I would dedicate myself to dance, learn new skills and prepare myself to fill those trademark boots when it was time.

Before I knew it, high school was here. Tryouts for the drill team were open to dancers in the 9th grade and above. I'd had five years of studio and competition experience to get me ready for the audition, and I nailed it. I'd be on the high school football field come next fall.

It didn't take long for my focus to shift. Now that I'd made the team, I wanted to be an officer. The next year, I tried out and made junior lieutenant, and I was thrilled! Until I found out that I received the second-highest score at the audition, just below the new captain. The school felt that it would be more considerate to let a senior girl be first lieutenant, since I had another year left of high school.

I thought *being a junior lieutenant is good, but being a first lieutenant is better*. Sometimes in our quest to get what we want, we fail to realize that everything isn't about us. I'm jumping ahead. That's another lesson for another chapter.

My attention shifted to what I hoped was next. Captain. The prominent placement on the field, the whistle, my name and rank announced over the loudspeaker at every home game all delighted me. But was that all?

Throughout my life I've struggled to see the beauty of where I am right now. Not what I'm working toward tomorrow or a year from today, but right now. Have you been there? It's so easy to rationalize this behavior by saying, goals are good or there's nothing wrong with wanting more. I just want you to consider this – how do you define more?

Think about the last time you picked up your phone for a little Instagram scroll. You follow the influencer who always seems to have the perfectly coordinated and trendy ensemble or the interior designer who shares nothing but stunning images of homes you could never afford. Or perhaps it's the fitness guru who got her body back two weeks after having four kids. You think it's mindless and entertaining, but how do you feel when you're done?

Immediately, I start to think that I'm not stylish or beautiful enough, that my home is run down and tacky or that I'm a lazy slob who can't seem to get her abs back because I'm just not motivated enough. Let me be the one to tell you – that's a lie.

You loved that dress when you bought it, the shoes and accessories too. Your home is lovely and warm and filled with your memories. Honey, that body is wonderfully made and worth celebrating.

Although I was happy to be a junior lieutenant, the nagging thought that there was something better prevented me from fully embracing the joy of that moment. I missed the opportunity to be proud that I had set a goal at nine years old and reached it by fourteen. Now, we do it to ourselves every time we get online.

I'll share a little secret with you. Most people, places and things you see online aren't quite who or what they're advertised to be. The beauty influencers are sent clothes curated by brands that want you to buy what they're selling. The makeup is selected for them too. They're all being paid to promote these products under the guise of an unbiased review. And do you know who's confused? You.

Despite all of the perceived beauty and perfection, these men and women still undergo countless procedures from minor to major because they are still unhappy with their appearance. Let that sink in.

```
It took me a long time
    to learn that the
good things in my life
   are actually great.
```

Looking back on my drill team days, I miss the sisterhood, the tough kick line practices in the August heat, the smell of freshly cut grass on the football field. Don't get me wrong, when I made captain of the Irving High School Toy Tigers, I made history. I was the first black captain of my Texas high school drill team. It was glorious, but the best part wasn't my name being called, dancing in front or even blowing that whistle to count us out onto the field. The best part was being a member of a genuine team.

The good stuff is what made that whole experience so sweet. Seeing my number posted on the sheet unveiling the team gave me a feeling that few things have compared to in my life. Locking pinkies was a thing as we circled up before performances. It was symbolic of the shared bond. The little things are what I miss now, what meant the most.

When you look at your life, what do you see? Do

you see all the good stuff you've been granted? I know sometimes it can be hard, but we've all got things to celebrate in our lives.

Maybe you have some amazing friends, but you'd really like a life partner.

Maybe you've got a great career, but you want to make more money.

Maybe you're in a beautiful home, but you want to lose weight.

There's nothing wrong with desires, but I want to challenge you to fully embrace the good stuff and resist the urge to compare your actual life to the life you think someone else is living.

Do you know how many people would give anything to have one good friend, let alone several? Think about how many people make a ton of money but have little to no happiness or fulfilment in their career? The safety and security of a home is likely much more precious to the person with the trim body you want than you even realize. What's the point? A posture of gratitude positions you to receive more and keep your life in proper perspective.

I haven't done this perfectly. Shoot, to be honest, I still struggle with this but I can enjoy my career even though I'm pushing to grow. I can love my husband and still pray that he closes the kitchen cabinets and drawers at night (ha!). I can accept that my body is healthy and strong while I work to build muscle and tone it more.

For me, the game changer was acknowledging that by comparing myself to an image, rather than a living, breathing, flawed person, I was robbing myself of my own humanity. I was robbing myself of my own joy.

We cannot get so busy looking ahead that we miss what's right in front of us. I like to remind myself that I'm experiencing the things I once prayed for. Are you? When you reflect on the things you wanted one, three or five years ago, do you have them now? What have you achieved already that you have yet to fully appreciate? That's how you get happy.

I am adamant about getting into a habit of consistent gratitude and appreciation because grief is going to come. When it does, you want to have a reserve of good days and good things and good people to draw on to pull you through. You're going to need it. I know I did.

Chapter Two

Talk it Out

THIS CHAPTER OF MY STORY may be the hardest to write. I remember the day vividly. It was June 18, 1995. Father's Day. That morning, I woke up early and marched straight to the kitchen of the duplex my mom shared with her younger sister. We lived on the top, and auntie lived on the bottom.

You see, it was a special day. I was going to make breakfast for my dad! Not just any breakfast, but a feast. We went to the store a day early. I picked out bacon, sausage, eggs and scrumptious bread for toast.

I should share that my parents divorced before I was five. Like so many children of the 90s, addiction gripped my family. When he was clean and sober, my dad was gregarious and warm, funny and kind. Drugs and alcohol brought out darkness and ugliness that scared and scarred me, but he promised me that he would show up today.

I'd fried the bacon in our biggest skillet, mashing down the bubbles to make sure each slice was perfectly cooked and crispy. My sausage had just the right amount of char on the outside and was grilled just right. I used softened butter to spread on the toast before I popped it into the oven, watching the door to make sure it didn't burn.

The crowning achievement of this fabulous feast was the eggs. Although my dad hadn't lived with us for years, I knew just how he liked his eggs. Three over easy, some of the edges cut off, heavy on the black pepper. He had no way to know that I had practiced countless times to make sure when the big day came, my eight-year-old

wrist could flip the eggs without cracking the yolks he loved to dip his toast into.

I did it, y'all! I changed into my new pink dress and prepared the table. Mom let me take out the good china and even use the cut crystal glasses for our orange juice. When you grow up in a less-than-perfect environment, you value those moments where things do feel right. However, it didn't last long.

I finished breakfast right on time, with five minutes to spare. The table was set, and dad would be there any minute.

The excitement was unbearable. I went down the stairs and sat on the front porch to see the moment when dad arrived for the best Father's Day breakfast in town. Those seconds turned to minutes. Those minutes became an hour. I worried that the eggs would be so cold, he wouldn't want to eat them.

Soon, I cracked the door and yelled up to mom. "Has he called?" I think by now you know the answer. Once an hour and a half passed, I decided to make some fresh eggs and toast. If I went and made sure everything was nice and warm, dad would show up, and all would be well.

I sat on that porch for more than three hours that Father's Day. To be honest, I hadn't thought about it in such great detail until now. It still chokes me up and causes my eyes to well up with tears. I was a little girl who wanted nothing more than for her dad to show up and spend time with her, pleased with her effort to make him feel loved. It was the start of a dangerous and isolating trend in my life.

I'm not sure when I became a perfectionist, but I believe I was born that way. There hasn't been a time in my life where I haven't taken comfort in completing a to-do list, finishing a flawless assignment or cooking a quality chef's meal.

My relentless commitment to getting any and everything right has served me well. In school, I was a straight A student, officer of the honor society, university ambassador and member of the dean's list. Excellence had its perks. Professionally, it was much the same. I'd prepare more, work harder, stay later and sacrifice in ways others wouldn't.

In the middle of the great recession, I was recommended for a job that wasn't advertised. I landed job after job, climbing the ladder of my field and excelling in ways that even I found hard to understand. The problem is, I never stopped to ask myself what I was chasing.

My heartache from growing up with an absent, often emotionally abusive father manifested itself in a few different ways. Instead of confronting the trauma of my childhood experience, I clung to the characteristics that my life continued to reward. Perfectionism. Detachment. Diligence. Humility.

Under normal circumstances, these aren't bad things to have. There's nothing wrong with wanting to do your best, protecting yourself emotionally, being dedicated to your work and keeping your confidence in check. For me, though, that wasn't it.

I was simply a shattered little girl still waiting for someone to show up and prove she was worthy of love and praise.

It took me some time to truly understand what was happening here. I spent years pouring myself into my work, refusing to let anyone get close to me and always wondering why I wasn't good enough no matter what I did. Then one day, I woke up.

Whew, therapy was rough at first!

I felt raw and naked and ashamed sitting on that couch, asking a complete stranger to tell me why no matter what I did, the emptiness inside wouldn't go away. Contrariwise, my therapist, let's call her Sarah, walked me through the deep work of acknowledging how much my dad walking away from our family, from me, wounded my heart and soul.

I want you to know, theres power in your pain, but you have to talk about it.

Faking it with a good façade can only carry you so far.

Sarah helped me see the threads that ran through some of the habits that kept me trapped in a cycle of despair, from how I weaponized my pursuit of perfection to the ways I built barriers around my heart and mind to make sure no one would hurt me the way my dad had.

Y'all, I wish I could say this was a cute, refreshing little exercise. Maybe filled with pristine Instagram photos of me journaling with a cup of chamomile tea, but it was crushing. I went from being the woman who never cried to one whose eyes poured tears like a torrential rainfall on a steamy spring day.

Here's what few people tell you: forgiving is hard and healing is harder.

In an instant, I can take myself back to that chocolate brown couch where my feelings were much more bitter than sweet. Sarah slowly helped me untangle the bramble of my painful past. Branch by branch, we lifted the veil on the baggage I needed to release to allow myself to find wholeness.

It sucked most days until it didn't. After eighteen months of no excuses, powering through the horrid homework and making my mental wellness a priority, I could see the sun again.

There was bliss despite my brokenness.

Deep down, we all have stuff. I'm not asking you to tell me, your best friend or your partner. My advice is simple; just be honest with yourself.

When I took inventory of how hard I was pushing, willing myself to be anything but me, I had to know why. Have you asked why you do the things you do? Are you willing to confront the reasons why especially when they're rooted in unhealthy thoughts or experiences? Don't waste years in vain justifying stuff that isn't serving you.

I spent years telling myself that excellence would fulfill me. What I really hoped was that it would ensure I was worthy enough of love and loyalty. That no one would leave me again, that I would have that table filled with food and joy for the rest of my life.

My father would have bouts of sobriety throughout my early adulthood. He'd continue to call me drunk or high, curse me and call me awful things when I didn't engage or indulge him and fail to show up the times when I wanted and needed him most. Guess what? It doesn't matter.

I was committed to my emotional work. You should be too. I'm here to say, share your struggles and your story with someone safe. Therapy was restorative and life-giving for me. Beauty can be created from chaos when you're willing to open up.

Years later, my father walked me down the aisle on my wedding day. That day the unhappiest little girl was the happiest woman in the world because I had finally healed.

Chapter Three

The Valley

SOMETIMES THE BIGGEST blessings in your life also come with the biggest challenges. Buckle up for this one, it's full of twists and turns.

My whole life, I dreamed of being a journalist. My mom is a news junkie, so the news was always on the television in my house. Sundays were a real treat because that's when my favorite show came on. 60 Minutes. That trademark ticking and the booming voice of the correspondents previewing their piece to start the broadcast still gives me goosebumps.

I was on the school newspaper and yearbook staff all through middle and high school. I was voted most likely to succeed in my graduating class. No pressure, huh? The time came for college applications. I only submitted three: Northwestern, The University of Texas and Texas Christian University.

Ultimately, I chose TCU. I'm a proud horned frog and couldn't wait to study at the Bob Schieffer School of Journalism. I followed the path prepared by countless journalists before me. With a major in broadcast journalism, I interned at two television stations before graduation and landed a job working for my dream team: The Dallas Cowboys. That experience is for a whole separate chapter.

Finally, I was hired as a weekend evening anchor in Sherman, Texas. The station was headed by a news director with big-market experience and a knack for finding talent. To this very day, he's one of my biggest supporters and someone I count as a mentor and friend. He made me promise to stay for one year. I made it to ten months.

If you didn't know, the starting pay in journalism is abysmal. The great majority of your producers, reporters and anchors have side hustles or second and third jobs to survive. I've even sold plasma a time or two to make rent.

When an offer to anchor the weekday morning show at the dominant, number one station in Tyler, Texas, I was thrilled. Not only was this a fantastic move up, the market had produced some of the best journalists in our field for decades. This was a phenomenal opportunity!

I'd work the overnight shift, from midnight to eight in the morning, ending my day by anchoring the broadcast. Things started wonderfully. The team seemed genuinely kind and happy to have me on board. A few short weeks in, though, things began to shift.

My co-anchor was named managing editor of the show. That's essentially a manager who ensures the quality and integrity of the broadcast. Initially, I wasn't bothered by this at all. My goal was to be the best anchor and reporter I could and help our station win the time slot. So, in my opinion, the title didn't matter to me.

Very quickly, people in East Texas warmed to me. We grew the morning viewership to record numbers, and I received countless requests to speak at and host events across the region. While I thought things were going great, my co-anchor believed differently.

He started showing up to work later, and later, his chatter during the newscasts became biting and condescending. When our station hosted a public event inviting viewers to the station, and it was obvious that I was a favorite for our community, things took an ugly turn.

My news director at the time began calling me into his office, accusing me of unprofessional conduct at work. I was incredulous, if I'm being honest. Those short meetings evolved into critical emails nearly every other morning. My news director hated my hair, my makeup, my voice, my presence.

During this time, I steeled myself. Each morning, bracing for the impact of whatever blows he would throw that day. Nothing I did would pacify him.

Then, I broke.

One morning, my co-anchor slipped a sharp insult into our banter. Unflinching, I retorted back with no humor or delight. It cut and I knew it. After months of putting up with him and his superiority, I cracked. I knew I was in trouble the minute we reached the commercial break.

Immediately, I received an email from my notorious news director. "In my office, right after the show."

I showed up on time, head held high. He had the sneer of a wild animal, relishing in the fact that his prey knew it was over for them. Then in a flash, he started his monologue. For the next ten minutes, he went on about what a terrible hire I was and all the things my co-anchor had told him I was doing every morning.

A puzzled look crossed my face because it finally clicked.

"Don't look confused," he spat.

The whole time I had worked at the station, the man charged to be my partner and operate as a leader in the best interest of the shift had been spinning a web of lies about me to improve his standing at the station.

I shouldn't have laughed, but I did. This is where I came out with my apology. It was wrong of me to lose my cool and expose a rift on air, regardless of the circumstance. Before he could cut me off, I continued by telling him that none of what he had been told about me was true.

I produced countless emails detailing my co-anchor's tardiness, mistakes, poor leadership and outright dishonesty. My boss turned beet red, flashed his teeth in an awful grimace and proceeded to curse me worse than he ever had before.

Have you ever had a moment where you feel as if you've left your body? You're in the room, but your essence isn't there. That's what happened in his office that morning. I felt sad but vindicated. I'd worried that I wasn't living up to expectations or doing my job well, when there was a calculated effort to disparage and discredit me.

This was not supposed to happen!

I got my dream job, only to end up in a nightmare.

That morning meeting was the start of years of abuse. From that day on, my news director would call me and spew such vitriol that I started saving the messages in case I needed proof of his conduct.

Imagine being a source of light and joy for thousands of people in your community as they start their day while living through the darkest days of your life and career. My long-managed anxiety flared up in an ugly way.

Most mornings, I would prepare in isolation. Reading and writing as quickly as I could, making sure there were no mistakes in the scripts. I was pleasant and prepared for every show. Then, a few months in, an announcement was made that my co-anchor was being promoted to the evening show.

Let that sink in. The very monster who was responsible for making my time at the station miserable was being elevated. I was flabbergasted. But I had no idea that a gift was on the way.

Unexpected gifts are often the greatest gifts.

That's how I described my new co-anchor at the station. He had a heart of gold, was secure and confident in himself and his skills, and we became fast friends. We shared devotion to our faith, quirky humor and a love of news.

We were truly a dynamic team. Our strengths and weaknesses complimented each other beautifully, and most of all, he was loyal.

When our news director tried and failed, time and time again, to get him to fall in the footsteps of his predecessor, he refused. I'm sure it came at a price and under immense pressure, but he never turned on me or made me out to be the person my previous co-anchor had.

The contrast was jarring. While my new partner was supportive and understanding, my boss was still relentless.

Some days, I would lock myself in the bathroom right outside the studio and rock myself until the panic attacks subsided. My heart would race uncontrollably, and I would ask myself how was I supposed to make it through the day?

The answer is simple, although it wasn't easy.

Focus on the things you can control.

A few things were true: I was prepared and passionate about giving people the news they needed, I was now surrounded by people who cared about and would protect me, and my boss would email or call me something hateful almost daily.

Can you count the number of times you've let something external interrupt your internal harmony? How many times have you allowed one bad thing to overwhelm the countless good things at your job, at home or in your relationships? We all do it!

Today, you're going to dial it in and commit to what you can control. It's normal and healthy to work and be better in some areas while appreciating how great things are in another.

That station is not a place that I remember fondly, but I have lifelong friends from it. What if I had retreated and punished my new co-anchor for the sins of the first one? What if I hadn't refused to let my former boss crush me professionally and emotionally? What if I hadn't developed the muscle to drown out all that noise and bring my best every day no matter what message or criticism I received? I don't know, but I do know that I want the same thing for you.

In the midst of chaos, you can bring calm to your life.

The craziness isn't always a sign that you need to make a move. In multiple moments in my life, I've found that hardship and conflict are more about you than the person engaging in it. The man in the corner office could have believed that he was punishing me for whatever perceived wrong I committed, but he was the conduit that brought me the greatest gift of my time at that station.

Happiness is a byproduct of my earned ability to not let what's happening outside affect me fundamentally inside. Because of this, I'm stronger for the struggle, and you can be too.

Chapter Four

From One to Two

WE WERENT GOING TO MAKE IT

out of the engagement. The sweet, overwhelming love we shared from the night we met was gone. I was sick of that man. He was sick of me. We might as well quit, I said.

Falling in love is really easy. Staying in love is really hard.

When people ask me about meeting Kevin, I tell them it was like electricity. There was a charge between us immediately that neither of us was prepared for.

I met my husband in the most unconventional way possible, at least for me. I worked as a morning anchor in a small Texas city, which meant that I would often host community events.

The Tyler Organization of Men asked me to serve as the mistress of ceremonies for its big event, an Apollo night. There would be about two dozen musical acts on stage at the Liberty Theater in downtown Tyler on Friday, February 21, 2014.

I should have known something was strange at the planning meeting. Well, I sort of did. As we went through the program and run of the show for the event, the organization president, Mr. Leroy Francis, kept asking me questions. These weren't questions about the program. He was asking things like…

Do you like living here?

What are some of the things you enjoy?

Are you dating anyone?

Now, when you have a public profile for your job, dating is complicated. I had just stopped dating another guy a few short months before this surprise inquiry, so my head and heart weren't really up for getting to know someone else.

But, there was something unique about the way Mr. Francis asked me these generally personal questions. He had a particular man in mind, and he even slipped up in response to one of my answers by saying, "Kevin says that too."

A couple of weeks later, it's the night of the event. It's formal, so I'm in full glam. (You know, hair styled, makeup done and high heels on.)

In walks this guy. Mr. Francis, the most affable man with the most heartwarming smile, beams and says, "Dia, this is Kevin. He's going to help you up and down the stairs all night." Insert my internal eye roll here. I mean, he was literally wearing a polo shirt and a blazer over it. Are you kidding me?!

Here we are. The event begins. Kevin takes my hand and walks me up onto the stage. That marked the beginning of a three-hour event, and I laughed nonstop. First, the man had no details about the evening whatsoever. But with every question I had, he found an answer. Second, there were older ladies and gentlemen performing, and Kevin was attentive the entire time. Every lady had his hand as they journeyed onto the stage. Third, he made me cackle until my sides hurt. We had fun like old friends even though we had met minutes before.

Only, it didn't click for me immediately. Kevin asked me if I wanted to grab dinner afterward with him and his friends. I declined. I'd been awake for nearly twenty-four hours at that point, and I was utterly exhausted. So, I promised we would exchange information and connect someday soon.

This didn't feel like he was asking me out on a date. It truly felt like two young professionals living in a small city linking up and creating a sense of greater community. Eventually, the event came to a close, and Kevin presented me with a plaque honoring my service, and just like that, it was time to go.

A small crowd of people surrounded me to take photos and chat. But by the time I looked up, he was gone. Don't get me wrong, I don't blame him in the least. It was late, and his friends were waiting for him.

I found Mr. Francis and said, "I told Kevin that my friends and I would get together with him and his friends. Could you please give him my number?" With his trademark smile, he replied, "Absolutely."

The next morning, Kevin texted me and invited me to meet him and some friends to watch some playoff basketball. I said no. We still texted and talked a couple of times. Then he invited me to a group hang out. Again, I said no. For some reason, I felt like I needed to be with him alone. The quick study he is, Kevin asked me out one more time to have sushi the following Friday. I accepted immediately.

Although initially, it felt like we would be friends, I saw something in this guy that I hadn't seen in all the others. When we were seated at the table, I immediately jumped in.

"Here's the deal. I'm twenty-seven years old. I have my own career. I don't need you to take care of me. However, I'm only interested in a committed relationship with the destination of marriage at this point in my life. If you don't want that, cool. But I'm not getting dressed up on a Friday night to be your friend. By the way, if you do decide to pursue a relationship with me, you've got twelve months to figure out what you're trying to do. I'm not saying you have to propose at that time, but you better have a plan. I refuse to wait around while you figure out what you want."

Y'all... I have no earthly idea where this came from. Was it honest? Absolutely. Was it a whole lot? Oh yeah.

Our butts barely touched the chairs at the table when I unloaded on this man I knew for all of a week. That wasn't the best part. The best part was his response.

Kevin looked at me intently and listened. He didn't flinch, wince or waiver. His eyes never left mine. When I finally stopped talking, he smirked. Yes, the man just smirked at me like he was amused!

"Dia, I'm not scared of you. What are you drinking?"

That's it! If I could have melted onto the floor at that moment, I would have.

It clicked. Right then. Kevin didn't respond to my soliloquy at all. He just accepted me and where I was at fully in that moment. Days later, I told him I would be his girlfriend. A short ten months later, he asked me to be his wife. On the first anniversary of that proposal, we got married in our shared hometown (isn't that funny) in front of more than 300 family and friends.

Let's talk about going from one to two because, like love, it can be beautiful but also push you to what you think is your breaking point. No matter how much the one you love loves you, they cannot make you happy. You've got to find that for yourself.

Falling in love with the man I firmly believe I was made for happened fast. It felt like I was floating through life. It was as though color never looked that vibrant before. Al Green talked about love and happiness, singing, "Happiness is when you really feel good about somebody." News flash: he was wrong.

You cannot ever find your happiness in someone else.

That's a complete thought, and I hope you take it to heart.

Placing the responsibility for your joy in the hands of someone likely struggling at times to find their own is unfair. Take it from me. It doesn't work either.

I should have seen the trademark signs that I was setting myself, and my darling love, up to fail.

We met when I was in a very unfavorable place professionally, emotionally and in some ways, spiritually. You can't control when you're going to meet your person, obviously, but you have to critically analyze how you're doing and feeling before adding another person to that orbit. I was volatile when issues or challenges showed up. That meant during some of our early disagreements, Kevin was walking over landmines to avoid upsetting me.

Conflict is healthy. The constant concern isn't.

Remembering the early days of our engagement, I described feeling stressed, but he defined it as fighting a lot. Ouch. No doubt, all the other unchecked stressors in my life led me to unleash on the person I loved most.

Dinner was my favorite time of day because that was our daily meal together. We'd hit all the best restaurants in town and fill up on everything from steaks to fajitas. Then, we had a moment.

It's a regular Tuesday, and Kevin came home from work. I was dressed up and ready to go out to whatever fabulous restaurant he had planned for the night. In my sweetest voice, I asked, "What's for dinner tonight?"

Quick as a flash, he spun around and said, "You better get in that deep freezer and take something out to cook."

Now, I had a choice to make. It was an easy one for me. I ran out to the garage, lifted the lid and yelled back, "Chicken or fish?" Be careful of the expectations, spoken and unspoken, you craft around your relationships. This isn't just advice for romantic relationships. This is for your coworkers, family and friends too.

The fact that I was dressed up and ready to go out before Kevin even suggested that we would be eating out that evening was enough. I was communicating an expectation that he potentially could have felt pressure to fulfill. Thankfully, I spotted this one sooner rather than later. I whipped up a nice dinner, and we had a great night at home.

What if I hadn't seen the error of my actions? Imagine how much harder I would have made it for him to balance his budget, make decisions independently or talk to me openly about his feelings. These things are all fundamental to the wonderful marriage we share today.

Enough of the good stuff. We've got to get into the bad stuff.

The night Kevin proposed, I suggested we get married at the courthouse. He scoffed and told me no way, because we were having a big wedding with at least 300 guests. It felt like the engagement party was planned before he popped the question. Then, Kevin asked me what I wanted to eat at said party and let's just say, it didn't go over well.

You see, the people in your life have dreams and expectations too. Want to know something ugly? I lost it at our engagement party. After I had demanded a million little things from the man I promised to spend my life with, I couldn't take it when he demanded this one big thing.. I was wrong. Here I was again, not checking my own emotional well-being before dumping my damage onto what should have been a beautiful celebration.

People are who they are. You know how I told you that Kevin never really responded to my list of wants, needs and priorities when we sat down to have that sushi? That hasn't changed. My husband has been a man of minimal words from the beginning, and he's consistent in that. Words are my thing. That's probably why you're reading my version of this story and not his.

I can't tell you the number of times I've desperately wanted my man to shower me with a monologue detailing the many ways he loves and adores me. It's not happening. That's not who Kevin is.

He doesn't close doors, drawers or cabinets.

The brother cannot put a cap on the toothpaste to save his life.

Walking across the bathroom floor with wet feet doesn't bother him.

Need his recipe for a dish? He doesn't ever follow one.

If you want to hold hands for a stroll, good luck.

Guess what: none of that matters. I've got a whole list of things I'm not great at, but he loves me anyway. Kevin accepted me completely from the beginning and chose to love me anyway. My goodness, that's the best part.

What's the lesson in love? It ain't enough.

Going from one to two doesn't make you complete; it shows you who you truly are. Marriage made me look hard at the components of my personality that need some... okay a whole lot of work. Our union has taught me how to take responsibility for myself. Whew, that's a whole separate story.

If you're unhappy in a relationship, think about what you're expecting to get out of it. The greatest gift is to be seen, appreciated and loved as you are. Everything else, my friend, is on you.

Chapter Five

It Ain't About You

SOME PEOPLE ARE JUST MEANT
to be in your life. One of those people for me is Stephanie. What's funny is, I met her husband first.

Our church needed some volunteers to work with the media ministry, recording service and putting together videos that would air during various events. Naturally, it was a good fit based on my skillset, so I agreed.

That's how I met her husband. Rosheon is a tall, warm man who loves to laugh. He ran the media ministry at the time, and for some reason, took an interest in learning more about me. At the time, I was getting back into my own relationship with my faith. In my early 20s, I was a young professional and despite what looked like a bright future ahead, I was wholly unfulfilled.

Since I lived close to an hour away from the church, making very little money as a new journalist, Stephanie and Rosheon took me in. I'd have Sunday dinners with them after service and find gift cards for gas slipped into my bible.

Let me take a moment to say, God bless people like these two.

I should probably tell you that I'm a Christian. I grew up non-denominational, went to a private Christian elementary school and like many believers, I had my struggles. The challenges and ebbs and flows of my life left me wondering where God was and how I fit into whatever His grand plan was.

If you're not a person of faith, that's okay! Hang with me here. I promise, I'm going somewhere. You don't have to be a Christian, Muslim, Buddhist or a member of any other faith to take something from this story.

We've all questioned where we belong in the big, wide universe. I bet, no, I know, you've longed to have certainty that your life has meaning in the grand scheme of your community and our world. Shoot, me too. That's why I was back at church for the first time in many years.

So let me tell you more about Stephanie and Rosheon. These two are ridiculous in the best possible way. They've been married for more than thirty-five years now. They go on bike rides together, mentor young married couples at that same church, and they literally light up when they're together. It's pretty disgusting.

Jokes aside, they radiate the happiness I've spent so much of my life working toward. Both seem to have this innate guiding light and resolve that keeps them strong and steady, by each other's side through some incredible high points and deeply sad low ones. I've watched them be faithful to God, each other, their family, and still find a way to love on, coach (or correct with a strong hand) and love on me.

Through the years, I've gotten closer and closer to Stephanie. Full disclosure, we're both Virgo women, which I believe is part of why she sees a little, tiny bit of herself in me. She's a dynamic professional, mom of two, looks amazing, never too busy to talk, funny and oh so real. Years ago, she cornered me and politely said that I needed to forgive my dad.

Ugh!

Immediately, my defenses shot up. How dare you? I'm not the problem. He is. He chose to drink and do drugs and abandon my family and me. I'm civil to him, which is more than he deserves.

In her quiet, firm way, Stephanie would simply repeat, "You need to forgive him."

I'm tough. Stephanie would never admit it, but I learn the hard way when things are emotionally challenging. My next series of questions, or attempts to be combative and prove that I was 'right' sounded like:

I'm nice to him. Why isn't that enough?

What do you expect me to do?

How can I love someone I don't even really know?

It had to be exhausting. In fact, ya girl is worn out just writing this. She stayed firm. It took a few months, but I finally surrendered. That's a big word, y'all. Surrender. It means to cease resistance. We'll come back to that.

Get the therapy! This is my second time saying it, but boy, was it helpful. I reached out to a therapist who helped me untangle all of my complex feelings around my dad, his addiction and his abandonment. She also blew my mind by helping me discover why I kept finding myself in some of the same traps throughout my life. It legitimately felt like a huge boulder had been crushing my chest for my whole life, and with every session, it would lift a little more.

I forgave him. I don't tolerate my dad. I love him. I see him fully, accept and love him with no strings or without keeping score. It may not sound like a big deal to you, but baby, I felt like I could fly.

I'll let you in on a little secret…

You dont know everything, even about yourself.

Stephanie saw how debilitating my unforgiveness was for me. Her own life experience and wisdom gave her a window into what held me back from a better relationship with someone I love. I didn't even think it was a problem!

You need to have people who have been in the place that you're in right now. I do mean safe, trusted folks who have a vested interest in your wholeness. Notice I didn't use the word happy here, because well, that's something entirely apart.

Through my own vulnerability and willingness to listen, no matter how much it hurt, Stephanie taught me more about myself than I could have learned otherwise. Who's in your corner? Who's speaking life into you, but more importantly, challenging you to get uncomfortable to grow?

I almost wished I could say the nudging stopped there, but no. My little lesson on forgiveness was just the beginning. But I will tell you, the first moment of self-reflection and forcing yourself to actively work toward healing and greater perspective was the hardest. This is a muscle you have to flex.

Once the thrill of getting married waned and the glow of new love subsided, reality set in fast. Kevin and I were two strong-willed, wildly intelligent, independent creatures trying to create a life together. Boy, it was rough! Real rough!

All of my married friends were new to the game, like me. I needed someone, anyone, who made it the distance (we're talking twenty years or more) to tell me the secret sauce. How the heck was I supposed to stay married to this man who wouldn't put the toilet seat down?

Enter Stephanie to always and forever save the day or save the marriage in this case. I called in distress, "I cannot with this man! He won't do this. He won't do that. I wish he would just listen to me because I know best! How do you get Rosheon to do what you want him to do?"

I'm exaggerating, but only slightly, here. I had lost my whole mind. My patient mentor burst out laughing. Her howls lasted more than a minute. Now, if you're in television like I am, you know that's a long time.

When Steph finally took a breath, she gave me a one-liner that changed my life, and I'm betting it'll change yours too.

It ain't about you.

I was livid. My face was hot and beet red. 'How can you say that?' I screamed. We talked for over an hour on the phone that night. She broke it down like a college thesis, looking at the biblical foundation of what marriage is and what it is not. Mostly, she used scripture to show me why I had the situation all wrong because of one thing: my perspective.

As a young wife, I centered myself at all times. It was almost as if I viewed myself as the sun, and Kevin, my coworkers, family and friends were designated planets designed to orbit me at my own sense of time and priority.

Before you judge me, you do it too. I'm just not sure if anyone has told you that before. In conflict, we're often mad because we feel wronged by the other person. In frustration, we only wish they would see what we so desperately want to communicate. In strategy, our priorities should be reflected in the actions of the group.

We want what we want, when we want it or we're unhappy.

Stephanie exemplifies tough love in my life. I know in my heart how much she loves me, but that compels her to push me to think differently. She taught me (and is still teaching me, to be honest) how to de-center myself and consider the people around me. It's a game-changer.

I've learned my dad was battling his own demons, which led him down the path of addiction. My mom always said, "He loved you the best he could." I not only know that, I feel that now. I've found empathy for him, despite my own heartache.

In my career, I've stopped taking things so personally. Sometimes you give it your all to get the promotion, but it doesn't pan out. That doesn't mean you've failed or that you're not in the right place. Maybe the leadership sees something in you that you've never considered. It could be they've got a position planned for you that's even better than what you were eyeing all along.

When it comes to Kevin and the toilet seat, look, I don't have all the answers. I've simply learned to stop and try to think from his vantage point. I'm not assigning meaning to things I don't quite understand or appreciate. I make it a point to ask questions and truly put myself in his shoes more often than not.

We have complementary strengths and weaknesses. When we're at our best, we're backing each other up and covering one another's blind spots. That's a strength.

Stephanie has shown me how to look inward when I'm feeling emotionally overloaded, frustrated or angry. I see the bigger picture in every area of my life. Today, I don't offend easily. I'm more understanding of others' feelings. My calculation and consideration in all things takes the people around me into greater account.

I'm at peace because I'm able to turn to God for my sense of place and purpose in a way that I wasn't before.

Now I'm less concerned about getting my way, because… it ain't about me. That was a huge step toward finding my happy.

Chapter Six

Bloom Where You're Planted

ONE BENEFIT OF BEING IN THE
job market during the Great Recession was it put me in
a position to land a pretty incredible job out of college.
Unbeknownst to me, The Dallas Cowboys were looking
for a new reporter to join their ranks.

In my senior year of college, I interned for a sta-
tion in the sports department that fall. Apparently, the
awesome sports anchor and reporter I worked under were
well connected and recommended the team consider me
for the role. I can't describe how nervous and excited I
was about this possibility.

They offered me the job! Not only would I be work-
ing when I graduated, but I would be working for Amer-
ica's Team: The Dallas Cowboys. Aye!

Day one was a blur. I actually started working a
month before I graduated from Texas Christian Uni-
versity. In my business casual attire, Chuck Taylors laced
with a smile on my face, I kept showing up eager to learn
and happy to work hard.

The Cowboys crew is the best there is. My boss at
the time, Scott, had news experience and hailed from
Miami. This man laid a foundation that took what I
learned as a student and shaped me into the journalist
that I am today.

"Let the people tell their own story. You're just there to fill in the gaps," he said. I live by that mantra as a storyteller to this day.

Each day brought something new to soak up. Since I started during the offseason, I went to work on the archives – organizing and cataloguing everything I could to make it easier to find old footage on the fly. The videographers painstakingly showed me where all the equipment was stored and how to properly take things out and put them back in order.

In the evenings, I would watch old Cowboys documentaries to get to know the history and the big games, plays and moments that made the franchise the envy of the world. While the team was building its strength, I was training my muscles too. My goal was not to be a star. From the onset, my goal was to contribute and be a valuable asset to the team that took a chance on a young woman with no connections straight out of college.

I've got a whole family at The Star in Frisco from the time I spent working for the Cowboys. You want to talk about a dream job? This was it! Sadly though, it wasn't my dream.

If you know anything about me, you know I love some Dallas Cowboys football. I'm a Texas girl, through and through. I grew up watching the 90s 'Boys win three championships under Jimmy Johnson, thanks to the triplets: Troy Aikman, Michael Irvin and Emmitt Smith. Sunday in our house was for God, football and food.

From the time I was tot, though, I wanted to be a journalist. I was the rare kid who knew what they wanted to do with their life really early and just so happened to be right. I wanted to follow in the footsteps of Ed Bradley and Gwen Ifill, not Pam Oliver or Michelle Tafoya. My dream was to represent communities that were often left out. Despite the thrill of standing on the sidelines of my favorite team, it wasn't the same.

But I had a job to do and I was blessed to have it.

It wasn't all-stars and touchdowns. These were some tough, hard-earned years of resilience, focus and determination.

Take the podcast. The Cowboys came in early with a show called, The Lunch Break. Shameless plug here – it's fantastic. The Crew, as we were dubbed, chat around the mics like a group of friends debating what we saw the past week and what fans can look forward to. I had a blast, but as the youngest host and the only woman… I got some spicy comments.

The guys all knew their stuff in and out, backward and forward, at every level. This was new to me. It felt like no matter how much I studied or prepared or tried to blend in, I stuck out. It was the early days of social media, but hateful folks have always found a way to break through.

```
When you feel like youre
up against impossible odds,
that doesnt mean its time
to quit: your breakthrough
   is on the other side.
```

The players were surprisingly fun, compassionate, and friendly. Part of my job was to get interviews in the locker room after practices and clip sound bites from those interviews for stories and content online and on television. I loved the creativity of it all.

I'm the only girl in my family, which means I grew up in my own locker room of sorts. I knew how to handle myself in a room full of men, and I refused to take any mess. Yes, I was young and less experienced, but I demanded respect, and for the most part, I got it.

For some reason, though, the fact that the players seemed to like me and grant me interviews that they wouldn't give to other people started causing suspicion. Players would pop into our office to say hello or bring me treats here and there. Mostly, the guys treated me like a kid sister. Then I got called in to speak with my boss. Oh boy.

Put yourself in my situation. I loved the Cowboys, enjoyed my job and the people I did it with, but I knew that eventually, I wanted to move on and start my career as a journalist covering news. Here I was, in trouble for my "conduct" and trying to defend myself against unfounded accusations that I was up to something nefarious or salacious with team members. My first instinct was to quit. Then, in a moment of clarity, I thought, I don't have to take this.

Looking back, I can't blame Scott. He was doing what he had to do. In over a decade with the team, he'd seen his fair share of young women come into the organization with goals that had nothing to do with working for the team. Plus, I walked into the facilities ready to learn the team history but had no clue about the culture and inner workings of the organization. I'm going to own that.

Chin up, I accepted his critique. It was valid, and I understood.

Ever been called into the corner office? How did you respond? Did it tank your day, your career with the company? Did you become resentful and resistant? Did you quit?

I didn't. I was just starting my career during the height of an economic recession, and I owed it to myself and to the Cowboys to learn from this and pivot.

You've got to bloom where you're planted and trust that you're going to shine no matter where you are.

So often, when we're working toward something, we discount the place we're in. I had a lot to learn. And this was the place I was positioned to do it. So, don't let a small disappointment or setback convince you that you have to pull up stakes and move.

Think of it this way; that professional critique was the first of countless in my career. If I hadn't taken Scott's advice to reflect on my own conduct and craft strategies to perform at a higher level, it would have been virtually impossible as a journalist.

The criticism from Cowboys fans pales compared to some of the vitriol I've received as a reporter and anchor. I had no clue that this was the preparation, building those muscles we talked about, for my next level.

My attitude remained positive. I leaned into best

practices and bought into the Cowboys culture. The very people I felt were unfair in their assessments of me initially, showed me step-by-step how to be better. I blossomed just like a flower in fertile soil. My confidence and capabilities grew, and I earned the opportunity to host the Jerry Jones show and report from the field live during the preseason games, right alongside some of the best in the business.

There were other pressures. A few of the players were more than insistent that I violate company policy and go out with them on dates. Every time, I declined. I'm not saying the right decision for me was always easy.

Wait, I never had any desire to date any of the players – period.

The hard part was knowing some of my coworkers did not believe I was standing firm on my principles, morals and upholding the company standard even when I was. I fought for my reputation both in my department and inside that locker room. But every day, I kept showing up the right way.

Life is funny. I was getting ready to interview one of the team's new first-round draft picks. This just so happened to be one of the guys who insisted that I go out with him. The photographer needed to run and grab an additional piece of equipment, so the player and I were seated and making some small talk. He proceeded to push, "Dia I don't know why you keep telling me no. You want someone else on the team? It's pretty annoying that you act so stuck up like you're better than all of us."

I only smiled. At that moment, the photographer

walked back in, and we finished the interview. The camera had been rolling during that entire exchange. I didn't know that at the time.

Minutes later, the same photographer who undoubtedly questioned my integrity with our boss and others on our team came to my desk practically in tears. "I didn't know," she offered softly.

Why do I share that story with you? It's to remind you of something my mom has told me my whole life: cream always rises to the top.

> Be your best no matter
> where you are, no matter
> who you think is watching.

I spent three years working for America's Team, and I loved it. More than ten years after my departure and it's still the number one thing people ask me about on my resume. I call everyone, including the folks who originally were skeptical of me, family. I like to say I grew up at Valley Ranch. Those years also taught me how important it is to have people in your life to lean on.

As the saying goes, if you want to go fast: go alone. If you want to go far: go together.

Chapter Seven

Create Your Crew

IT WAS A NORMAL WEDNESDAY
morning. Kevin was making breakfast, and I was getting Alina, our daughter, dressed for dance class. By now, our baby boy Evan had arrived. He was almost eighteen months and a few handfuls of energy and love.

While I was getting Alina's leotard on, Evan looked up with a completely blue face and grimaced. Not a second later, he collapsed onto my chest.

My heart stopped. I screamed, "Kevin!" My husband grabbed our son, flipped him over and hit his back, assuming something was caught in his throat. Fifteen seconds later, Evan popped up like nothing had happened.

I stripped the leotard and tights off Alina.

Kevin ran next door to grab our neighbor, a nurse.

Ann sat with Kevin and our son while I got Alina dressed.

Then it happened again. Evan, completely blue, collapsed onto my husband.

We called 911. Paramedics rushed into our front door in under four minutes, but just like the first time, Evan was alert and walking around asking for a snack already.

All his vitals were perfect. They told us to take him to the pediatrician in the middle of a pandemic, which meant that only one of us could go inside. It was me.

The pediatrician was concerned. We were transferred to the emergency room.

More tests, more tears, more questions.

My hands are shaking while writing these words. You cannot fathom the terror of a toddler who collapsed twice with no certain cause.

In private, I cried long and hard – deep sobs sung out from my chest. There's no worry like the worry a mother has for her child. What happened to my son?

I couldn't eat. I couldn't sleep. I wish I could say I prayed, but I couldn't even do that.

Then, my people showed up.

Our culture is at a crossroads. The global economy has created an environment where more and more young professionals relocate to cities they know nothing about, strictly for their careers. Fewer of us spend less time in places of faith. Social media means we can be "friends" without ever meeting for a quick coffee or lunch.

We are more disconnected than ever, but support starts with connection.

My mom tribe refused to let me go at the biggest scare of my life – questions surrounding my baby boy's health – all alone.

The mailbox overflowed with cards that spoke to me in ways that were tough to quantify. And still are. We got so many gift cards to local restaurants that I didn't have to worry about what we would have for dinner for weeks. And one day, my phone rang.

It was Bernie. And Bernie is one bad mama. Her only child, a grown daughter, is her pride and joy, and

Bernie makes no bones about it. She's engaged, enthusiastic and always there.

That one day, I was sitting on the floor of my closet in the dark, trying to gather myself enough to get on with the day. It was a short call that started with, "Dia, this is Bernie. I'm calling to ask how you're doing."

I crumbled. So often for moms, the focus is your children, without fail. I was in crisis, too, though. As a new mom, I had no frame of reference for managing something this big and emotionally draining. "I'm struggling because I'm scared, and I don't know what to do. All I want is for my baby boy to be okay."

In a flash, Bernie pulled another mom onto the call, and she prayed for me. I don't remember the words, and it's not as important as what I felt sitting on the floor of my closet. I felt surrounded. I felt supported. I felt strengthened.

The kindness shown to my family in those days, weeks and months Evan was under evaluation by every medical expert in neurology, cardiology and pediatric health care were life-giving to us. We needed a true tribe of people around us to hold us up when we felt like falling.

I have no doubt that without each and every one of the people we are fortunate to call part of our extended family, the experience of going through that episode with Evan and all the unknowns after could have crushed us. There's no substitute for having an authentic community around you. I needed it around me.

Evan is doing great! He's a big boy now, making

his presence felt in our home, bringing every one of us immeasurable joy. Ultimately the doctors couldn't point to a single cause for the scare, but it hasn't happened since. We believe that it was a fluke, and he's going to continue to be a perfectly healthy and happy little boy.

When I think about how I could stay happy during all of this, I go back to that call. My people showed up. They didn't need me to put up the bat signal to alert them that I was in distress or that my family needed their support. In a real relationship, the people you know, know you.

Who shows up for you?

Where are the people in your life who pray for you when you can't pray for yourself?

When your people ask how you're doing, are you honest?

I did not sleep for months after Evan collapsed. Those few seconds felt like a lifetime. We bought special monitors that would alert us to his breathing patterns overnight. I never let him out of my sight. It got to a point where at just fifteen months old, he started telling me to "go."

The mamas in my life coached me through each step, little by little. They shared their own stories of scares with their kids when they were younger and offered up secrets to stay sane during it all. Not only did they show up, y'all they walked alongside me.

Are your friends for you when its not fun?

I'm normally the life of any party, always ready with a perfectly-timed joke, but not then. I was stressed and exhausted to the bone, but they all stayed close. It can be tough to ask for help. Thankfully, my friends made sure I never had to ask.

You have to forge those friendships when you don't need them. Want to ensure when you're unhappy that you have some serious help on the journey to get back happy? Prioritize people.

I check on my people. I spend time with them. I pour into them when they need it. I don't do those things looking to benefit. I do it because I love and care for them. In a community, when one cup is empty, you have a lot of other cups to pour a little from to fill it back up.

My mom friends put me back together after a very broken season with my son. But you know what else they taught me? ... that I was trying to do too dang much.

Chapter Eight

Health is Wealth

I HATE RUNNING. Okay, hate may be a strong word, but every image that comes into your mind when I say running doesn't apply to me.

When I got my first pair of running shoes, I envisioned myself jogging along downtown streets with my ponytail swinging perfectly in the wind as I bounced up and down. My arms would glide alongside my body, and my tummy would be tight, firm from all that cardio. Ahhh, fitness.

The reality, though, was ugly.

Getting myself to the gym for my first class was pretty involved. There were so many things to consider. I'd reached those dreaded thirties, and I felt much older than that physically, from years of not prioritizing an active lifestyle. Who wants to be struggling and embarrassed in a group class? Also, which class should I take?

Ultimately, I settled on a class called Tread. Think of it like spin class, but on a treadmill instead of a bike. The instructor was named Patrick, and he was a real runner. The guy stood 6'2" and had a head full of thick, lush brown hair that he'd have to swoop out of his eyes from time to time. His energy was infectious! For forty-five minutes, every Tuesday and Thursday, Patrick would coach us through a series of sprints, hills, intervals and workouts.

It was brutal, but I loved it!

"Set your treads to 6.0," he'd yell. "Go to 7.0 if you're feelin' fine!"

I'd automatically set my treadmill at 6.0 because I wanted to set my expectations nice and low. Patrick was notorious for running around the gym, checking on every person in the class, correcting form and making sure we were 'feelin' fine' during the workout.

One day, I honestly couldn't tell you when, Patrick started bumping up my speed and incline during Tread classes. He'd come over with a motivational chant, and before I knew it, I was flying that much faster.

My takeaway from that part of Tread class: you're stronger than you think.

The irony of that one group fitness class was that it scared me. Every time I hopped onto my tread for the day, I'd have butterflies in my stomach. Patrick was a great coach who could see something in my insecure stride that told him I could handle more, and he was all too happy to give it to me.

This was a serious shift toward taking care of my body because I wanted to be healthy and strong. My mind was clearer. My clothes fit better. And my energy was through the roof.

I'm not here to tell you that you have to start running. I am here to tell you unequivocally that you have to make your health and wellness a significant priority in your life. This is not an edict to drink wheatgrass smoothies, take hundreds of supplements and hop on whatever diet is all the rage right now. This is simply a gentle nudge to share how one shift has helped shape my life and my sense of joy and how much I want that for you too.

In the words of Forrest Gump, "I was running!" I didn't reach the point where the runs themselves were fun, but I liked the things that came with them: endorphins, less bloating, decreased stress, I could go on.

Something powerful happens when you commit to your physical well-being in a major way. That desire grows. I started with running, but soon after, I aligned myself with eating more healthfully.

I don't believe in diets… for me. I'm a big fan of carbohydrates of all forms and fashion, I've never seen a slice of cake I wouldn't take a chance on and, since we're keeping it real, I love wine. What I do believe in are balance and discipline.

While my primary motivation in getting back to working out was my overall health, I wanted to look good too. I'd be lying if I said otherwise. It felt counterproductive to go hard in the gym and down nothing but cheeseburgers and tacos at mealtime. I've been there!

It started small. I gave up something I felt was manageable: soda. My chronic acne started clearing immediately. Okay, I liked that.

Next up, meal prepping. Our lives are busy, and if I was going to keep myself and my husband on track, I needed to make it easy. I started preparing meals for us both, twice a week. Kevin lost thirty pounds in a snap. Alright, now, I was ready to keep pushing.

Then, we got pregnant.

When I tell you we fell off the wagon, I mean…

we fell off in grand fashion. Celebrations galore consumed our calendars, featuring our favorite foods. The sheer amount of cookies, cake, pasta and chicken wings we ate in the months leading up to becoming parents was mind-boggling looking back.

I'd like to stay married, so I won't tell you how much weight Kevin gained. Thanks to genetics and my slim frame, I gained twenty-two pounds during our first pregnancy. I stopped running about midway through, but I walked instead. October 2017 brought my greatest pride and joy. My heart grew in ways that I didn't believe were humanly possible before. I was a mom.

Life happens, and in all the best ways sometimes.

As your life gets fuller, it can be even harder to prioritize your health. My days were packed with breast-feeding, pumping, diapers, swaddling, working, snuggling and unadulterated, pure love. Suddenly, I didn't matter as much anymore, and that was fine by me.

What is it for you? Did you land the big promotion that came with a more significant cost or commitment? Maybe you have some family struggles that require more of your time than usual? If you're in emotional distress after losing love or a cherished friend, I get it.

Life happens, and in all the worst ways sometimes.

What I want you to consider is how much you're worth it. Loving your children doesn't have to come at your own expense. No job is worth sacrificing your own well-being. Family is incredibly important, but there are only so many hours in a day. Your mental health and stability are tantamount to that same security in any other area of your life.

You're worth it.

You're worthy of the investment to spend fifteen, twenty, thirty, forty-five minutes or more to get active. It's transformative in ways you may not understand. Take a hike, sign up for that group fitness class, do a little yoga at home. What you do doesn't matter as much as doing it does. Showing yourself the same care you extend to others isn't selfish – it's smart.

When you dedicate some time to make a few meals and snacks that are tasty and healthy, you're saving time, money and giving your body what it needs to serve you well. I mean, fast food tacos may be good going down but after that… it's all bad! All my random Chipotle pick ups and DoorDash deliveries are gone, and my bank account and body are much happier!

Those minutes when I'm jogging away, ticking off my mileage for the day, my mind is clear. The stress and pressure of whatever I have to face that day are gone. It's my meditation. I talk to God. I pray. Feeling my heart beating hard and strong is a reminder that I'm alive and well. Plus, nothing compares to the satisfaction of a run that's over.

Our family has an active lifestyle. My daughter will never know the word 'diet' because we simply share what's healthy and what's not. I'm proud to plant seeds for her and my son to grow strong and well. My kids also know that when I'm on a run, "It's mommy time!"

I've lost any baby weight from the two pregnancies we had, less than two years apart. Most of my favorite clothes still fit, and I don't feel bad about saying that I love the way I look again! I'm healthy and strong, mentally and physically.

Listen, I am no trainer. I'm just a woman whose life changed a lot in a short amount of time and who had to figure out her new normal. My home and the people in it are happier and healthier because I decided to make my own wellness foundational. If I can do it, you can too and do it in your own way.

I just got off the treadmill before I sat down to write. It was three short, sweaty miles in 75% humidity at 6:30 a.m. I'm midway through training for my first half marathon, which I plan to complete before I'm the ripe young age of thirty-five. If you had told me on that first day of Tread class some six years ago that I'd be where I am today, I would have laughed in your face.

Start small. Take one step. You never know how far the course you chart now will take you. Want to be happy? Getting healthy and well is guaranteed to clear your mind and make it easier to find your own slice of joy.

Chapter Nine

Some for You, Some for Others

I JUST SPENT A WHOLE CHAPTER talking about prioritizing yourself. Now, I'm going to tell you what we have to do for others if we want to become our happiest.

My mom is named Anita. Picture a petite black woman with pecan-colored skin, high cheeks and a knowing smile. That's my mama. She embodies strength, resilience, support and most of all, unconditional love.

Growing up, my mom raised my two brothers and me by herself with no assistance from our dad. But she was never angry or bitter, despite the raw deal of being a single mother who had to put her own dreams down to set us up to go for our own.

There has never been a moment or a milestone that my mom was not present for. I cannot recall a single time in my life where I was being honored, celebrated, or showcased when Anita was not sitting in the audience with that trademark smile on her face. I'm grown now, and I know a measure of the price she paid personally to be present for my brothers and me.

My mom made sure I had a new dress for every occasion, which is why she spent so much time at her sewing machine. When I was a little girl, I couldn't wait to visit the fabric store and pick out the material, buttons, notions and trim that would be stitched together for a creation nobody had but me. Boy, the fights we would have over every detail. Selecting the pattern, considering the time it would take to sew, you name it.

As a kid, I was an overachiever. I guess you could say I'm still one today. I mention that fact to illustrate, I was involved in a lot of school and extracurricular activities. There was never an awards ceremony where I didn't hear my name over the sound system to come to the stage to receive a certificate.

Mama practically lived at that little Singer sewing machine, which would be humming late into the night to make sure my set was flawless. Talk about love.

She would sew homecoming dresses, dance costumes for entire teams I was part of, even my prom dress my senior year of high school. Mom never complained. She never seemed tired. She was always happy, ready and willing to do whatever it took to make sure I felt confident and beautiful.

Anita is the epitome of sacrificial love. Who or what do you love like that?

Some of your life is for you, but some of your life is for others.

During my dancing years, I'd mentor and work with younger girls to help them master skills. Oh, the thrill of watching a child realize a goal they've been working toward for weeks. Helping to shape their ability and aptitude while reinforcing how special and incredible they are is one of the most rewarding experiences of my life.

When I started my career, I wanted to volunteer

weekly as a way to get to know people in my community and help in an area of great need. That led me to Meals on Wheels.

I'm a big fan of the elders in our world. They hold life experience, wisdom, compassion and a sense of identity that I find invaluable. So many of them need help, though.

Food insecurity is a big deal for people getting older. Not always living near family as the cost of living continues to increase is difficult. That broke my heart, so I decided to pick up a couple of routes once a week.

To start the shift, we'd make up the meal kits. I'd arrive at 10:00 a.m. as we portioned out proteins, carbohydrates and a little sweet treat. The crew would add milk and maybe a bread option, then the drivers started rolling through.

It was a blast! We'd listen to old school R&B. I'm talking Earth, Wind and Fire and Frankie Beverly and Maze as we made up each cooler for all the fantastic volunteers who spent their time, energy and gas driving around our community getting food to some folks who needed to eat.

I had quite a few favorite clients. Mr. George was a World War II veteran blessed with a family who lived in the metro. He owned a beautiful home in Kansas City's Hyde Park area, and often, I would see his daughter sitting out on the porch with him as I strolled up with his dinner for that day.

Sometimes, he would share stories of how much the city had changed both positively and negatively. Other times, Mr. George told the tales of his time at war. He choked up once talking about a dear friend he lost during combat, who died in his arms. I saw him get red and flustered arguing about the horrible cost of war while defending American ideals and his devout patriotism. Mr. George was special. Mostly, we talked about service and why it was foundational to him. In his view, serving others was the highest honor whether you were military or not.

One day, I showed up ready to pack my meals and hit the road. The director pulled me to the side as I threw the strap of my cooler over my shoulder and said, "Mr. George passed away this weekend." I froze. Emotional, I shed a tear.

I knew he had advanced cancer, but he always seemed so energetic and alive. Now he was gone. The director reminded me that he was surrounded by his family and people who loved him, that he was gone to a better place without the pain and suffering. It still hurt.

I'm not sure Mr. George knows what an impact he made on me. I learned more about our nation's history and his generation in those weekly visits than any history book had even shown me. If I ever felt too proud that I spent a couple hours a week delivering meals in my neighborhood, I thought about how he spent his life serving our country.

What do my mom at a sewing machine and an Army veteran have to do with my happiness? I'm so glad you asked.

There is joy in sacrifice and serving others.

Both of them showed me that.

On days where I questioned my self-worth, I could draw on the fact that my mom spent her whole life making sure I could shine. She gave up her full night's sleep, so I could rest easy. That easy smile of hers came from a sense of love. Mom, to this day, will tell me that those sacrifices brought her immense joy even though she was confronted with impossible odds.

Being able to pour into someone you love despite your own sadness, disappointment, or hardship is a secret sauce y'all. Not only was mom able to escape that for moments at a time, but she also cultivated a whole new identity and reality for me. I was a happy, content, resilient child, thanks to her. I had no idea the hidden battles she was facing because all I saw was her love and happiness in me.

Mr. George took that to another level. It's one thing to serve the people you call family or friends. Imagine that level of selflessness for your country and people you will never know. Here I was, thinking that I had mastered the art of volunteerism, but I had so much to learn. That porch and the many conversations we had sitting on it gave me a greater perspective on my life's purpose.

Take a minute and think about the people closest to you. How have you gone out of your way to serve them well? Do you get up early or stay up late so they don't have to? Are you willing to do more so they can do less?

Trust me when I say it's a surefire way to invite more fulfillment into your life.

Let's go a step further. How are you serving your community well? What are you passionate about? Start there. I promise, and I don't generally like to make promises, that one hour a week dedicated outward will instantly uplift you inward.

Suddenly, my problems seemed a lot smaller in the scope of a man who, on the surface, did everything right and was still dying from cancer. Getting to experience deep gratitude for the everyday heroes in my own neighborhood was the antidote to discontent.

My love for my mom became that much deeper. My compassion became so much more potent. When you get outside of yourself, you'll see the people serving you more clearly and it'll inspire a more significant commitment for you to serve others too.

Those days driving up and down the street, helping people who needed it, are what I call happy days.

Chapter Ten

Speak Now

IT WAS A THURSDAY. I know this because we had gotten home the day before. My lifelong dream of becoming a mom, and not just any mom but a girl mom, had been realized.

Alina was perfect. You know how newborns come out, wrinkly with blotchy skin and baby acne? Not my girl. Our daughter was stunningly beautiful from the very first photo ever taken of her.

I went into labor at work. Don't judge me. With a few short weeks of paid leave, I wanted to spend every second of my time off the job snuggling and caring for our first child.

Toward the end of the pregnancy, my back was shot. I mean tore up from the hips up. On Sunday, I was reading a newscast, bouncing on one of those oversized exercise balls to relieve the pressure on my poor back. Then I felt it – a small gush of fluid.

Something in me knew that it was a bit strange, but I had to make a calculation. With less than an hour to go before the show, there was no way a fill-in anchor would make it to the station in time. I wasn't in any pain, so I decided to push through (no pun intended) and get through the newscast.

The minutes crept by like thick molasses syrup

coming out of a jar. Slow. Discreetly, I cleaned out my fridge and rummaged through my desk for anything that I may not want to leave behind for three months, but I still wasn't sure it was go time.

I got home and hopped in the shower while Kevin was sound asleep, snoring into the night. This was perfect. I needed to process on my own. The hot water was relaxing, and the pressure was just right. Then I stepped out of the shower, and there it was – another gush of a warm, clear liquid that I knew wasn't coming from my bladder.

"Kevin," I whispered softly as I nudged him rhythmically. "Kevin, tell me I'm tripping." He stirred, and I explained what had happened the last three or four hours.

"Call the doctor!" He screamed as he jumped up and started throwing on his clothes. Before I knew it, he was packing the car up with the bags I'd prepared for the hospital a few days prior.

"Dr. Hurt," I started as I talked to the on-call doctor that overnight. By this point, it was around 1:00 a.m., and for some reason, I felt terrible for calling and interrupting her night. More on that later in the story.

"Your story sounds pretty good, Dia. You should head to the hospital. I'll let them know you're coming."

I trash-talked my poor husband the whole half-hour ride there. Everything from there's no way this baby was coming then because first babies take forever to how embarrassed I would be if it was a false alarm. Kevin, the stoic saint he is, kept on driving.

We made a pact that we would not tell anyone that we were in labor until it was confirmed because people already answered the phone in anticipation of the announcement that baby girl was on the way. There were two emergency c-sections that early morning, so by the time the resident came to check on me and determine if it was time for Alina to make her entrance, it was 5:00 a.m.

I'm so ornery, I told Kevin as we parked at the hospital, "Leave the bags because we're not staying!" Welp. The resident reached down, came back up and not a moment later told us, "Congratulations. You're going home with a baby."

"What did he say?" I asked.

I was shocked. You know that when you're some thirty-seven weeks pregnant, a baby is coming soon, but I didn't feel ready. Sure, the bags were packed, and the nursery was picture perfect, but I had to give birth.

The good news is, I wasn't in any pain. Let me brag on myself here: I'm a strong woman. Things were moving in a blur all around me. The paperwork was filled out. Kevin somehow retrieved the bags from the car. The nurses moved me to a birthing room. We called our parents and let them know it was time.

I could hear the wonder and joy in my mom's voice.

You know how you watch those movies where women are sweaty, screaming and grimacing their way through birth? Not my experience, hallelujah. Physically, I felt fine. Emotionally, I was freaking out.

All the preparation we made – the birthing classes, the special tools and shower shoes, were all left packed away. My labor went lightning fast.

Around 5:30 a.m., the resident confirmed that I was in labor.

By 7:00 a.m., we were moving to a delivery room.

Once the clock rounded 10:00 a.m., it was time. Kevin was swamped trying to alert people at work that he would be out of commission because we were in labor. I told him to call the nurse. It was time to push. He had a confused look on his face that any other time may have been endearing, but right now, I needed him to move.

"Call the nurse. It's time to push," I repeated firmly.

Kevin dropped everything onto the couch and called the nurse. She popped in and I said for the third time, "It's time to push." Here we go, another puzzled look. Are you sensing the theme here?

"I just checked you a few minutes ago, and you're only at a six," she said. Six meant six centimeters dilated. The medical staff likes for women to be at ten centimeters dilated to start pushing.

"Ma'am, I've never had a baby before," I pleaded, "but I'm asking you to please check me again."

The nurse refused. She refused, y'all!

I don't back down.

Again, she denied my request to check my cervix.

To give you some context, this is the part of birth when you get down to the nitty gritty. The pain is at its peak, and your body feels as if it'll split into two any second. This is a message for mothers everywhere: make sure you have a partner, doula, advocate fighting for you to ensure your voice is heard during birth. It can get real during delivery.

My husband stood up, and with his deep, full, baritone voice, he commanded the nurse to check me as I had asked. Kevin, thank you for that.

The nurse begrudgingly dropped down and started to measure. Her eyes widened to cover half of her shocked face. "Oh my gosh, she's twelve centimeters dilated," she yelled at full volume to anyone in earshot on the labor and delivery wing.

Never have I ever seen medical staff move that fast. The door opened and shut in such rapid succession, it sounded like a drumline on the field at the Friday night football games I went to as a kid.

That same nurse now had to get in position to potentially "catch" my baby girl. Yup. The very woman who didn't believe me or respond to my repeated requests was now tasked with bringing my child into this world safely. The irony!

Shortly after, a resident entered the room, and the stress level for the staff decreased. Then, Dr. Hurt, the friendly on-call doctor I woke from her slumber earlier that morning, popped in. "Good thing you decided to come in, huh" she joked. "Now ain't the time, Dr. Hurt," I laughed.

When I tell you, the medical team tried to convince me not to push until my amazing obstetrician Dr. Ryan arrived, I mean it. The tables had turned, and they were the ones pleading.

I vividly remember looking over the railing of my birthing bed and telling my husband that not pushing wasn't an option. I grabbed my knees and pulled them as close to my chest as possible, then Dr. Ryan came running in to save the day!

Two masterful pushes, hey, I need my due on this one, and Alina Grace was born.

Giving birth is one of the most magical and miraculous things I've ever experienced. The tiny baby that grew in my womb came out bright-eyed and stunningly beautiful. Alina took my breath away.

She cried, and in a flash, Kevin said, "Hey." Our daughter looked directly at her dad and stopped crying. When Dr. Ryan nestled my baby girl onto my chest, I felt God's love. My eyes are flooding with the same emotion I felt that day as I write this.

After birth, the golden hour occurs when the medical staff goes away, the machines stop beeping and our little family soaked up each second. She was warm and alert, with the most gorgeous chocolate brown eyes watching her mom and dad curiously.

We left that hospital as a family of three, full of glee and started our new lives at home. It was a major, gargantuan shift.

The young couple who enjoyed late-night drinks and spontaneous dates now spent the days nursing, pumping, diapering, swaddling, doing laundry and waking up every two to three hours. I'm naturally a little anxious about new things and unexpected challenges, but this was stress on steroids.

I'd prepared as much as I could. Shamefully, I can admit that we took four birthing and parenting classes, I read a dozen or so books, and I had a master schedule for our first two weeks with a newborn.

Ha! It was a mess!

Kevin's parents came immediately, arriving shortly after Alina was born. So not only did we have a brand new baby, but we had family in our little townhouse too.

They went to get groceries. They went shopping. There was a completely separate agenda outside of my carefully crafted schedule, yet I juggled everything that came with becoming a mom. I felt so overwhelmed and alone.

My body had been through nine months of pregnancy and birth. I'll spare you the details of breastfeeding, but some parts can be painful to start. I wasn't sleeping. New babies need to eat a lot, at random times, no matter day or night. There was also the delirium of finally being a mom to a precious child that I wanted to be a perfect mom for.

Here's where I messed up: I never articulated to the people around me what I wanted and needed my experience to be like.

I needed time and space to settle in and gain some confidence and routine before we hosted family and friends. I needed my husband to provide balance in my ridiculous (y'all, it was too much) schedule and expectations that set me up to feel disappointed, even on the best day. I needed stillness to enjoy those moments of reflection and joy.

People cannot meet desires that you dont express.

I'm a natural people-pleaser. As an empathetic person, I'm specifically tuned to pick up the feelings of those around me. This is a good thing when you manage it well.

I remember thinking, this is Kevin's pregnancy too. It's his parent's first grandchild. This is a big moment for them. He deserves to have his support system in place.

When you're always focused on what everyone else needs, you neglect the things you need.

Six months in, I was drowning. It felt like the months were a blur. I felt unfulfilled and unseen in what I thought would be the best time of my life. I broke down and told Kevin that we had to talk.

It was a tough, tearful conversation. I explained how hard this entrance into motherhood had been, the emotional and physical toll it had taken, that I felt like everyone else's needs eclipsed mine and how I wanted things to change moving forward. I'm grateful for my husband. He really listened.

I just wanted the chance to be the mom I always dreamt of. I apologized for not sharing my heart sooner.

> **When youre vulnerable,
> it opens people up to
> truly hear you.**

It was like a switch flipped. Kevin became the parenting partner I hoped for. It was there all along! You simply can't get what you don't ask for.

Today, I get time to think before we make commitments and decisions regarding our littles. If we need some space, he supports that and advocates for me just like he did in the delivery room.

In my fear of hurting our family and friends or disappointing the people I love, I was hurting and disappointing myself. Are you doing the same?

Don't mistake this for making a case to always get your way. It's not that. This is a call to express yourself and your wishes upfront. I've applied this at work, at home, with friends and family. Do we always agree? Nope. But the people around me know where I'm coming from and why I feel the way I feel before it becomes an issue.

When it was time to give birth to our second child, the nurse immediately prepared for a quick delivery because my obstetrician informed her of our first experience. Why? I let her know that I was not pleased with being disregarded the first time. I set expectations for what our next birth would be like. Dr. Ryan wasn't offended. In fact, she applauded me and came alongside us to make sure it happened. It was great!

After Evan Reese arrived, my mom didn't visit until he was two weeks old. What a difference a little time made! I was out of adult diapers, into a rhythm with his sleeping patterns and actually able to have a hot cup of coffee most days. I was able to enjoy hosting our family as we celebrated our new addition. Everyone was good!

What areas of your life do you need to speak up in?

If you're anything like me, maybe it's a few. Process

your feelings and desires through the prism of your own needs. Get vulnerable. It's amazing how freeing it can be to let go. That's how you get happier. Speak now, so you don't have to hope things change later.

Chapter Eleven

Get Used to Getting Uncomfortable

OH MY GOSH, I GASPED. We had been trying for months, and now we were pregnant! Kevin was out of town on business, and I was jumping up and down in our bathroom like a madwoman.

Planning the perfect pregnancy reveal for my husband, who pushed harder than me to start our family, was so much fun. I ordered the cutest little chef's outfit with a hat to match and paid the exorbitant $20 rush delivery fee. How long could I hold a secret like this?!

I packed up the box with our positive pregnancy test, the adorable infant ensemble and a note that read: Baby C is cooking! (We both love to cook, so this was brilliant in my book.)

I set up a covert camera to record his reaction and, the man was clueless. It didn't help that he had been traveling nearly all day, exhausted from the work week, and I couldn't wait until the following morning. In my impatience, I broke down and yelled, "We're pregnant!"

Kevin was pumped. We set up our first appointment and got to hear the tiniest heartbeat. Holding hands, we walked out washed in the knowledge that we would be mom and dad. A couple of weeks later, we surprised our parents and a few close friends with the monumental news. Oh, the joy we both felt and were surrounded by.

Then came a day. I honestly don't recall which day of the week it was. Just that I woke up and something wasn't right. Immense pain was radiating from my abdomen, signaling that something was seriously wrong.

There are times in life where things do look like they do in the movies.

Screaming.

Crying.

A pregnancy gone.

Emergency room doctors confirmed the tragedy we already knew. We had a miscarriage one day shy of the coveted twelve-week mark that is supposed to indicate a pregnancy that's safe and secure.

What did I do wrong? I asked if it was my diet or my workout regimen, if I could have done something to save our never-born child.

The next day we were due for an appointment. When we saw Dr. Ryan, she asked, "How are you doing?" I cried, "Not good." She wrapped me in her arms and told me that I didn't do anything wrong, these things happen, and I could still have a baby one day.

Logically I heard the words, but I couldn't accept them.

For an entire week, I toggled between deep sadness, rage and fragility. I yelled to God more times than I care to count. Call me naïve, but I never understood how someone could love a child they never got to hold until that period of my life. From the moment I saw the positive test to the second I heard the sound of the heartbeat, that baby was mine.

Crushing is defined as an overwhelming disappointment or embarrassment, and I felt both.

When youre in immense darkness, it can be hard to imagine seeing the light again.

In one of our many conversations about how we would piece our hearts back together, I told Kevin I needed some time. One miscarriage does not mean that you will have another one, but the thought of it was too much for me to bear. I assumed a little space would help me heal.

He disagreed.

Kevin was resolute in knowing that we wanted a family, and this heartbreak wouldn't define us or be the end of our journey. I'm thankful for his vision. Uncomfortable and scary as it may have been for him, he determined that we needed to keep going.

Pain pushes us to process things incorrectly.

I was emotionally raw and damaged from a dream I viewed as dashed. Gone. Our doctor and every test told us that I was in perfect health and could carry a pregnancy.

We got pregnant the next month with Alina Grace. Her name means light. Not only was our daughter the light that brought me out of the crushing darkness of our miscarriage, but she's a breathtaking example of God's grace in that season. I love my baby girl! Alina was meant to be our first child. I know that in my soul.

Sometimes we have to be hurt and keep going anyway.

Sometimes you'll be disappointed and keep going anyway.

Sometimes you'll be disregarded and keep going anyway.

Get used to getting uncomfortable. The greatest joys in my life often come once I push past my discomfort.

So often, we shut down when things get difficult. I'm going to push back and ask, do you want to stay where you are right now? If the answer is no, allow yourself to feel, but get back up.

Everything in your life is meant to be used as fuel on your flight to new heights.

I cherished my first pregnancy, but the next one I coveted. I found a new appreciation for every day, appointment, milestone and sign that it would make it. My husband and I were hand-in-hand every step of the way, connected no matter what the outcome would be.

My eyes were wide open, y'all.

We can easily fall into the trap of sleepwalking through our days, not fully appreciating the wonder we're surrounded by. That crushing pain reoriented my perspective.

Be scared and do it anyway.

What are you putting off because you aren't ready to put yourself out there? Discomfort doesn't mean you're on the wrong path. It's just the opposite, I would argue that means you're headed in the right direction.

I often ponder, where would we be if I hadn't pushed through?

Don't rob yourself of a fulfilling future, ruminating over a painful past.

I can't promise you a perfect life, but if mine is any example, you've got some great days ahead, and you want to be there, not here.

Happiness is the delight I see in my daughter, knowing all we went through to bring her into the world. Your happiness is waiting for you, too, as soon as you push through those things that make you uncomfortable.

Chapter Twelve

Give Yourself Grace

IF YOU'RE READING THIS, you survived the COVID-19 pandemic. So, prepare yourself for a soapbox moment here.

A once-in-a-century global pandemic shuts down the world, and people were on social media shouting about how to live your best life. Stop it. No, stop it.

Hear me when I say you deserve all the honor and praise for surviving. You didn't need to thrive, get to the best body you've ever had, or shake up whatever industry you work in or revolutionize your kid's education. We made it. Hooray.

Part of the problem of this generation is we have access to so much information and curated content from influencers' lives who claim it's "authentic" and we end up measuring ourselves by an impossible set of metrics. I need to run that back.

We are measuring ourselves by an impossible and imaginary metric.

In March 2020, our daughter was two and a half, and our son was nine months old. We had someone who watched our children at home while Kevin worked from home, and I anchored the news from the station. When COVID-19 came crashing into our country and our consciousness, it caused some chaos.

Reliable child care was a challenge to come by. We couldn't count on our sitter to show up, and the schools that didn't close were booked with waiting lists a year long. What are two working parents supposed to do?

I can't even imagine tackling a real curriculum at home with kids who are bored and overstimulated from spending all day looking at screens while worrying if you can keep up with your full-time job to keep food on the table and a roof over your heads.

Don't get me started on the people posting snarky comments on social media about how parents just don't want to spend time with their own kids. It's enough to make you mad, sad and more stressed than you already are. We mean well, but why did some folks post perfectly-styled whiteboards of their "balanced" schedule for the day? Who took time to snap pictures of organic, home-cooked meals three times a day?

Confession: we got fitness watches that same month. Kevin insisted that when I was sent to work from home at the height of the coronavirus spread, we would make it count and get serious about some of our weight loss goals. We walked. I ran. We meal prepped. I tracked everything.

I was posting everything too.

Work was complicated. I never imagined that I would be anchoring the news from my basement for months. It was isolating and extremely challenging. Our daily face-to-face meetings became faceless conference calls. I didn't see any of my coworkers for weeks at a time. Interviewing people via Zoom versus visiting them in person became the norm. The energy and authenticity of what I liked to do was gone.

It would be wonderful to tell you that I came up with some revolutionary workaround to meet my company's content strategy and share stories that were transformational to our community, but that just isn't true. I did some great things, but most days, I made it through.

I'm part of several service organizations dedicated to volunteerism and community advocacy. Each group has a requirement, a standard, for how we serve. I won't tell you how many, but we spend dozens of hours each year tending to the needs of the most vulnerable around us. Financial obligations did not decrease, nor did the expectation that we would achieve the same goals despite the complete shutdown of the country.

Let that sink in.

Not every organization, job or person is going to get what I'm about to tell you so listen closely.

In the midst of a once in every 100-year crisis, it's cool to coast. I'm here to tell you one simple thing:

Give yourself grace.

Shoot, every minute of every day of every year... give yourself grace.

When I tell you I saw new blogs, businesses, non-profits and ideas spring up all over the place – I mean it. Part of that I believe is wonderful, but too many of us feel the need to prove that we're doing well.

While some of us are showcasing how well we're

doing, someone else feels like they're failing. I just told you, I posted sweaty selfies after almost all of my runs. Innocent, but that could be the basis for someone else dumping on themselves for not doing the same.

Protect your peace.

I was listening to a parenting podcast once, and the host said you can't manage more than three big rocks at a time. By big rocks, she meant priorities.

That stuck with me, and I've applied that to a few areas in my life: myself, my marriage, my children, our home, my career and my volunteerism. In practice, this is what it looks like: right now, I'm working on eating better, setting aside consistent time for myself and finishing this book, to be honest.

In our marriage, we workout three times a week in the mornings before the kids wake up, enjoy a breakfast date every Friday morning and have our business meeting every Sunday night. We're spending more time together, being productive and having fun with each other.

With the kids, it's potty training, chores (yup, they clean up their own play areas and rooms as toddlers because I'm not Cinderella) and eating well. Anything that falls outside of those big three is not a major focus for the family right now.

Professionally, I'm setting boundaries, not working outside my working hours (much) and insisting on coverage that gives me satisfaction.

Doesn't that sound more manageable?

Everything can't be the most important thing!

Now that I've got some structure and guard rails around my life, I don't feel bad when I see other people killing it in whatever areas their own big rocks fall into.

Oh, you're launching a business right now? You go, girl!

You've lost 100 pounds since the pandemic started? Wow, what an inspiration!

I can't believe you taught your two-year-old to read! Fantastic!

Those ain't my big rocks. I concentrate my celebration around the things that I've committed to and those alone. I give myself grace because I can't do it all at the same time. We also aren't designed to do that.

What thoughts are creeping in, creating a lack of contentment in your own life?

I can't answer that one. Only you can. I can challenge you to tailor this method to your own life and circumstances right now and reap the benefits of more balance and a heck of a lot less guilt.

We're trying to do too much.

If you've decided the time is right for you to step out and launch your own start-up, do it. I'll be right here cheering you on. I'd suggest maybe you wait to take over homeschooling the kids until the business is open and running.

If you're focusing on your fitness, hoping to lose weight and prioritize your health, that's great. Maybe doing that amid job loss and financial strain isn't the best time.

Talk to and think about yourself the way you would a friend.

My self-talk can be brutal. I internally interrogate myself about why I'm not eating better, working harder and doing more. I can let the comparison trap suck me in and suck the joy out of my own messy, beautiful life. What about you?

You're doing so much better than you think you are.

It sounds small, but the three big rocks made a big difference in my daily life. My goal isn't to tick off a list of achievements and measurable goals that I've achieved as the years go by. That doesn't look like happiness to me.

Happiness is having the wisdom to know what's important and finally fully committing to having a lot of fun too.

Chapter Thirteen

Don't Forget the Fun

THE SMELL OF PAGES TURNING
in a brand-new book is intoxicating to me. I've read a ton of non-fiction titles that stuck with me for years after, but a fabulous fictional story is my jam.

There's nothing like the tale of a headstrong woman who overcomes incredible odds or a mystery that keeps me reading late into the early-morning light. I just love a good book. My love affair with literacy started early, too, at the local public library.

Getting that first library card was a huge accomplishment for me. I could check out up to ten books at a time, and your girl knew how to push the maximum. Every Saturday, mom and I would make the trek to book heaven and scroll through all the latest, greatest titles.

Mom's favorite book is *Little Women*. She saved me a beautiful, early-edition copy that was one of her most treasured books. Anita is a bibliophile. My whole life, I've been surrounded by hundreds of books, from anthologies to biographies, and a twisty-turning thriller. But *Little Women* was the one story she couldn't wait to share with her only daughter.

I hated it. Mom was crushed!

Listen, I just couldn't get with the whims of the four

sisters and all their trials and tribulations. It wasn't interesting or relatable, or fun to me. Blah.

We argued back and forth about that book for months. I kid you not, months. This was the start of something I really appreciate about the power of the written word: debate.

Reading a book is like peering through a window into a new world. You can learn about people, places and things you've never seen and feel like you're in the same room with them. Great literature comes off a page like a worldly destination waiting to be explored. For a kid who grew up wanting to escape so often, a book was my first-class plane ticket out of reality.

All throughout my education, mom read every book we read in school. Every single one. We debated them all: *The Autobiography of Malcolm X*, the merits of my favorite president Thomas Jefferson, *Black Boy*, *The Color Purple*, *Pride and Prejudice,* and so many subjects and books that I can't begin to list them all. I got to know my mom and myself through reading so much. I plan to do the same thing with my littles when they get older.

When I started evaluating what I enjoyed and what made me happy, it was putting my nose in a good book. What's funny is, Kevin and I used to take road trips fairly often. He would drive, play his music or talk to friends, and I would read. To this day, he brags about the fact that I can read four books on a weekend trip.

Why did I stop?

What have you stopped doing that you love to do? Why did you stop?

I'm betting we have some similarities here.

We stop doing the things we love because we incorrectly assess that something or someone else needs our time and attention more. They don't!

You need you!

It's not about what you do. It's the feeling it gives you. When you plan your day and forget the fun, you rob yourself of the ability to restore and rejuvenate.

I knew I had a problem when I hit my lowest point, and Kevin asked me, "What do you like to do for fun?" In that exchange, I had no answer. How do I not know what I like to do for fun? That's easy; life.

I went from being a single professional with a bright future ahead, planning girl's trips and spa days, to a wife and a mother with two kids under two, all within a five-year span. That's a whole lot of change.

When time got limited, I limited my fun.

I didn't have time for a girl's trip because I had to save my paid time off for the wedding, honeymoon, maternity leave and maternity leave again less than two years later.

Who can afford a spa day when you're paying for child care for two kids, diapers, clothes and all the other stuff. Children have too much stuff y'all. Okay, let me refocus.

There's no way I can read a book when I'm barely getting enough sleep. 100 pages or 100 winks? Umm, that choice seemed simple.

Those decisions were to my detriment.

Prioritize what pleases you sometimes!

Earlier I joked about getting back to running, but I enjoy that. The ancillary benefits are my decreased stress, increased toughness, stronger heart and lungs, tighter tummy (aye!) and the sense of accomplishment for crushing a goal.

Mom and I are back arguing about books again, and I love it! Who doesn't love reconnecting with someone they adore in a new or renewed way? There's nothing like challenging my own thoughts and preconceived notions around a story or a subject that we've dived into through a book. I've even shared some titles with friends who find those moments when they can steal away and sink into a beautiful book are healing. I'm working with a friend to finally launch a small book club for teens to teach them the same passion for literacy I have. That's a fantasy I've held close to my heart for years.

My sewing machine is humming steadily too. I learned to sew at my mama's knee as a child. Now, I'm spending some late nights crafting cute costumes for my own baby girl just like she did. There's peace, purpose and a sense of legacy in that. You want to talk about what makes me happy? This does. Although Alina is already a more opinionated and judicious critic than I ever was!

I'm doing things for me, and it brings me wholeness and happiness too.

One of my favorite hobbies is writing to my children. Sometimes on days when I feel extremely low, afraid or unsure, I write to them about it. When I got pregnant with Alina, I told her how much I loved her and would do everything in my power to bring her into the world where I knew she belonged. She will read that one day and feel her mama's heart wrapped around hers despite my fear then.

I wrote to Evan when we were in the terrifying middle of his health scare and told him that he mattered and was a gift unlike any other no matter the outcome. He's going to read his mama's words about his strength and bravery when even the grown-ups around him were fearful. My son will see the names of the people who came to me in crisis to pray that he would overcome whatever obstacle he may have been facing.

I'm the fun, light-hearted yet serious, confident, balanced, tender and devoted woman my husband fell in love with those years ago. Today, I feel good inside and out. I've got the energy to run after the kids and the resolve to buckle down when we have a busy or slammed schedule. I dress up for date nights and make sure my man knows how much I adore and appreciate him.

The mood swings and erratic ups and downs of my temperament flare up from time to time, but overall, I'm level. Love radiates from me again. I can consider and be kind, gentle to the needs of others because I've done that for myself.

> I love the people in my
> life well because I love
> myself well.

I'm sowing seeds that are coming to harvest from having some serious fun. These are the things that make me happy, and I've discovered that they're making the people closest to me happy too.

Chapter Fourteen

Small Stuff is the Good Stuff

THIS GIRL HAD THE GUMPTION
to plant a garden. Not just any garden, either. I drew up plans for a two-level raised bed, complete with feet and a plastic liner to keep the wood from rotting too soon. I purchased a wood stain to give it that modern tone we like and made sure it fit in with the exterior of our home.

I built it. It was fly!

When the time came to plant, I was pumped. We live in the Kansas City area, and winter here lasts about 300 years. I've seen snow as early as October and as late as May in our time here. It's appalling, really.

Anyway, the time had come. No more hard freezes in the forecast, and I'd picked the plants I wanted to nestle into the soil that now filled my fabulous raised bed. Cabbage, red, yellow and green bell peppers, jalapeños, onions, broccolini, kale, spinach and butter lettuce, for salads, of course. I planted rosemary, basil, cilantro, parsley, thyme and a big pot of strawberries for baby girl.

The minute the plants were planted, Alina was asking, "Where are my strawberries?" The mind of a three-year-old, right? There are two lessons in this, but to recognize the obvious…

You don't reap the rewards of everything you do right away.

Sure, we all get the thrill of trying something new. You could be planting a garden of your own, launching a project at work, starting a new wellness plan or just becoming more intentional about your friendships. But you can't harvest plants that haven't grown yet. That doesn't mean your efforts were in vain. And if you ultimately want to pluck juicy strawberries from your plant, I would offer that...

The small stuff is actually the good stuff.

Look at it this way; planting or sowing that first seed is only the beginning. I'm barely a novice gardener, but when you talk to people who plant every season, there's a host of small steps they take to get a significant outcome in the end.

Are you fertilizing? What elements are you adding to the soil to make sure the environment is right?

Do you periodically pull the weeds? When you see things that don't belong, that threaten the ability of your plants to thrive, do you pluck them out?

How often are you watering? Rejuvenating and refreshing what you're doing is vital to keep your garden growing.

It's the small stuff, y'all.

I was ready to harvest too! I couldn't wait to toss a salad with greens fresh from my garden, drizzling it with homemade herb vinaigrette I whipped up using my own dill and parsley. Just like Alina, though, I needed to slow down.

Believe me when I tell you, there's a slice of joy in getting in your garden in the early mornings as the birds chirp and the sun is struggling to rise. It's a quiet time to reflect, connect with nature, express gratitude for another day and assess what your growing plants need.

I've killed a lot, I do mean a lot of plants in my day. I never had the focus or the patience to be successful in years past, let alone enjoy the weeks of work to get one or two plants to live. You know how I cracked the code? Instead of looking toward the harvest as the reward, I found satisfaction in the small daily tasks.

Watering is fun, pulling the weeds is fun and taking a breath here and there to see my work paying off is fun. Gardening and all the little chores that come with it make me happy.

My daughter was so busy looking for the big, ripe berries that there's no way she could enjoy the fun of being with her mama, spending quality time at work in the backyard. She's only three, so I asked myself, what was my excuse?

Don't search so hard for the big stuff that you miss the little wonder all around you.

What are you growing? Are you so focused on the end result that you're missing the beauty of the journey to get there?

The kids are a great reminder of this for me. Evan is almost two now. He's already a toddler. We won't have any more babies come home from the hospital. I couldn't wait until Alina was out of diapers, and Evan will be soon too. Boy, the laughs we've had during our diaper years, though!

This boy of mine refuses to eat vegetables at mealtime, and if you think a toddler can't run a house, you haven't met mine. One day, he will, though. For now, instead of me getting angry, frustrated and worried that he'll never choke down broccoli like the rest of us, I record his antics to show him what a riot he is.

Marriage is kind of like that too. We aren't perfect, and we don't pretend to be. I can tell you honestly, though, that our marriage came alive the minute we made the small things the big things.

Breakfast once a week may not seem like much, but when we both keep showing up no matter what else we're juggling, it's a sign that we matter most to each other. When my husband gets up early with the kids because I had to work late the night before, that's not small. It's huge. The nights I pretend to enjoy the random shows or movies he picks out, that's true love y'all.

Don't get so busy that you miss the beauty of the simple things.

My garden is thriving not because I hope and pray for a massive harvest at the end of the season. It's thriving because I make it my duty to tend to the small steps proven to make it successful and appreciate each milestone along the way. That's my mantra for life.

I can't tell you why you picked up this book, but I'd guess you're searching for a slice of happiness of your own, right where you are. It's not always easy. I can't see what you're going through in this season of your life, but I know in my bones there's something small worth celebrating in it.

Stop, slow down and open your eyes to whatever youve got around you.

Is the sun shining on you? Do you have a stable job and the ability to provide for yourself? Are you healthy? I wonder if you have one person you call a true friend?

All of these are small things worth celebrating.

A delicious meal that was made thanks to my hard work in the dirt is great, but time spent with my growing girl is so much sweeter. The tiny pockets of time, watching her learn about soil and fertilizer and what water can do, is the good stuff. I don't want to miss that part. It may feel like your fitness, professional, financial and other goals are the best part, but they aren't.

What are you watching on your way to where you're going? That's a huge clue into why you may be the unhappiest one in the room.

Chapter Fifteen

What You Do, Not Who You Are

ALL I WANTED WAS TO MAKE it as a major market news anchor and reporter. By now, you know that I've dreamed of being a television journalist practically all of my short life.

We've journeyed through my Sunday evening showtimes with mom, my first gig out of college with the Cowboys and into the tough, grooming years in my early news career. It's time to talk about what it felt like to reach the top and want to jump.

I started in Kansas City at a station as a morning reporter. Getting here was a story in itself. Taking things back to Tyler, I knew that I had to leave. Staying and signing the second contract they offered me was not an option. My mental, personal and professional wellness hinged on stepping out and leaving that chapter behind.

Let the job hunt begin.

I sent resume tapes to stations all across the country. It was the first time I had another person besides myself to consider when it came to where I landed. Kevin was going to move with me.

Did I skip the part where ten months after we met, he proposed to me at my mom's house? I'd informed him a few months into dating that there was no way we'd be leaving the small East Texas town together unless we were getting married. By March, the wedding date was set, and a venue was secured. It was happening!

Getting everything you want won't stop you from the pressure of keeping it.

Broadcast journalism is a brutal business; ruthlessly competitive and humbling for the most talented among us. Practically no one was calling me to set up interviews.

My whole plan rested on my ability to secure a new job making more money in a city where Kevin could fly in and out of town to his consulting job. Then my email finally pinged.

In Roanoke, Virginia, a station wanted me to come out and interview for a weekend anchor position. It was a larger market and better pay, so I accepted the offer to visit.

It felt off from the moment I made my connection in Charlotte. I had to board a tiny, twelve-seat plane to get to Roanoke. The plane rocked and swayed so much, I was physically ill when we finally landed after the short, thirty-minute flight.

The news director was impossibly kind and accommodating, thrilled to have me consider working for him. He showed me around the quaint town, which was beautiful and calming in a way. People were relaxed and friendly at every turn too.

When I walked into the station, my breathing stopped. It was small, no bigger than the station I worked at in a much smaller city. The equipment was outdated, the crew looked rundown and stretched thin, even the set had seen better days. All of this was fine. I could manage,

I thought. Once the time for the news meeting arrived, I realized this was not the place for me. There was very little to choose from. Whether it was weather, government or breaking news, I didn't feel any enthusiasm for the day or our duty to inform and inspire.

It felt like the second I arrived at the airport to leave, the tears started to flow.

Betting on yourself is scary, y'all.

By the time we reached Charlotte, I had crafted a new plan. There was a station in Kansas City where the news director had reached out a couple of times. I liked her immediately, but the station didn't have any openings for an anchor. Suddenly, with time running out and knowing that I had to make a move, my priorities looked a heck of a lot different than when I started my search.

We hadn't corresponded in weeks. I took a shot anyway, sending the news director an email asking her if there was any job open at her station. Within an hour, that news director had responded and booked my trip based on the limited window of time I had to make a decision.

There was only one problem: to even take the interview in Kansas City, I would have to turn down a guaranteed job offer in Roanoke.

Wheels were turning nonstop. My mind ran through every scenario, possibility and hiccup. I formulated plans from A through Z and still felt afraid to do what I knew needed to be done.

I let the news director in Roanoke know that I would not accept the offer. He was sad and confused, which I had a hard time swallowing. It had to be done.

When you have to choose between convenience and certainty, what do you do?

The night before my interview in Kansas City, I was up all night. Oh, the prayers I prayed, hoping that I'd made the right decision and wouldn't end up compromising all the wedding and life plans Kevin and I had made.

"It's going to work out no matter what happens tomorrow," Kevin assured me.

He convinced me to roll the dice on this opportunity. It's so important to have a strong support system when you're unsure. They give you the push that you can't always give yourself.

I went into that interview focused and ready. It was also one of the first times in my career where I was completely myself. I had nothing to lose. By lunch, the news director told me that she would be offering me a job. She just didn't know which one yet.

This may sound strange, but I could have cried at the table. That news director had no idea that I was out of moves and potentially out of the news business, if I didn't get this job. She couldn't have known that this was the first decision I'd made in my life that defied logic on the surface. I can only say she threw me the life raft I needed just as the tide was starting to take me under.

Meet my foray into the radical idea that my life was much, much more than my career. Kevin and I were getting married no matter what. He would be with me for life – job title aside. My faith was the strongest it had ever been. Truthfully, that's what got me to say no when I knew the Roanoke offer was off.

How many times have you said yes, knowing the right answer was no?

What's kismet is how quickly your life gets on the path you truly want when you let go of how you thought it would happen.

I started as a morning reporter, six months later, I was elevated to a night reporter. Six months after that, I was asked to take the weekend evening anchor job, which I did proudly and committed to another contract to continue.

Then, another shuffle. In a matter of months, I was offered a weekday early evening anchor job the week before I went on maternity leave to have our second child. Once I returned, a month later, I was interviewing to become the primary evening anchor at the accidental station I showed up at five and a half years before.

So much of the life I've shared with you in these pages has happened in those weeks and months. Professionally, I've thrived too. Why did I tell you that? It's because I desperately want you to know that you can thrive too.

I came to Kansas City in need of a job. What I've realized since then is that once I let go of the long list of expectations I had for that job, I was able to fall into the course that wasn't charted in advance.

A bad day didn't mean that I was bad.

Not getting picked for a promotion didn't mean that I wasn't talented.

I built an entire existence outside the confines of my career.

My unhappiness had deep roots in leaning on my job to bring me a sense of identity, purpose and joy. You can spend so much of your education, energy, time and focus on achieving that you forget who you are outside of that career.

Your job title cant tell me who you are.

Now, this is all wisdom I discovered after the fact. In the middle of my process, I was panicked and terrified that I'd made a major mistake.

Release the idea that a misstep in your career is going to cause your life to fall apart. When you do that, you're taking pressure off yourself and giving yourself permission to have different priorities outside the 9-to-5 grind.

What you do is not who you are.

Sounds counterintuitive, right? If my journey has taught me anything, it's that any measure of success and happiness is not linear. You can't spend your days obsessing over the theory that if you input X, you'll achieve Y.

That's why I was miserable before.

I put too much stock into one facet of my life: my career. I wasted countless hours trying to plot out the perfect course to reach the perceived top. I assumed that if I did all the right things, I'd get all the right results.

When you stop and strip all the aspects of your life away: who are you? At my lowest points, I couldn't answer that question. Can you?

Think of it this way:

**When your days are done,
what will people remember?**

Nobody puts their job title on their headstone. Nevertheless, years of service are rarely a footnote in the history of any human being. It's the people you love, the moments you share, and the joy those bring that make you happy.

I'm not trying to sound like I don't care about what I do. In fact, it's the opposite. I believe my career is my calling. In every sense of the word, journalism is my passion. However, I've learned to keep even that, in proper positioning in my own life.

What I do, isn't who I am.

That knowledge was one of the most fundamental steps to finally finding out how happy I could be.

Conclusion

The Happiest One in the Room

THE VERY IDEA THAT you're reading this makes my heart sing. This project is the most personal one I've completed to date. Although some of the details in these stories have been slightly altered, this is me.

I want you to know that I'm still discovering who I am and that rediscovery will never end. The very thing that used to scare me most is uncertainty. Now, I embrace the idea that I will always be in progress, and that's okay!

Through these highs and lows, I've gained a new-found appreciation for everything I've experienced and all the blessings that I have. My default posture is one of gratitude.

Please don't liken me to a therapist, or a preacher, because I'm neither. I'll never purport to have all the answers or keys to life. I would hate for you to walk away with the idea that I'm coming from a place of superiority.

I'm sharing my own stories from the lowest places in my life, just hoping it gives you the push and perspective you need to make it through on your own.

One other thing: I'm still unhappy sometimes. I refuse to leave you with a false positivity that every day will be packed with sunshine, rainbows and unfettered joy. But I did bring the fun and whimsy back into my own home, marriage, career and spirit.

- Be encouraged.
- Remember, you already have it all.
- What you think is so much better likely isn't.
- Talk the hard stuff out with a professional if you need to.
- Keep looking up, even when you're down in the valley.
- Getting something great can mean great challenges too.
- It ain't always about you.
- Bloom in whatever soil you're planted in right now.
- Don't forget to create your crew.
- Your spiritual, mental, physical and emotional health is truly your wealth.
- Some of your life is for you, but some is for others too.
- Speak up and share your needs.
- Get used to getting uncomfortable because that's how you grow.
- Give yourself the grace you'd give a friend.
- Fun is freaking fundamental, so have some!
- Small stuff is really the big stuff, so try not to miss it.
- What you do is not who you are. You're so much more.

I promise I don't have all the answers because I'm still figuring this out. What I do know is this: I'm the happiest one in the room now, not because the room changed, but because I did.

Acknowledgements

I want to express my deepest gratitude to the countless people who have shaped me into the woman I am today. My family: Anita Wall, my dearly departed godmother Cathy Breashears, my mostly sweet brothers Dale and Daniel, countless family and lifelong friends.

Thank you to my dad, James Wall, for never giving up.

I'd like to give special appreciation my professional family for being a source of support and strength through all the evolutions of my life and career.

Most of all, I want to thank my wonderful husband Kevin for pushing me to complete this book and share some tender parts of my story. You are the greatest gift, my love, and I thank God for you every day.

To my beautiful children Alina and Evan, everything I do in my life is to create a better, fuller and happier life for you. Mama loves you infinitely, forever.